SELF-PUBLISHING GUIDE FOR INDEPENDENT AUTHORS

HOW TO WRITE AND PUBLISH YOUR OWN BOOK

ANTHONY EKANEM

Contents

Preface

If you have ever dreamed of writing and publishing your book, you can realise that dream through self-publishing. Self-publishing is the route many writers choose these days to make their works available to the reading public. Self-publishing today is different from what it used to be many years ago when authors had to spend a lot of money to publish their book. Today, authors can self-publish their book for free or for as little as $100 depending on the self-publishing platform they choose.

As a soon-to-be author, the first thing you need to do to self-publish a book is to know your genre. One of the rules of writing is that you should write about what you know. If you have a specific genre that you enjoy reading, the chances are that that is the genre you will want or like to write about. Consider your interests and the types of book that you read before you decide on the genre you want to venture into. Your primary aim of writing a book should not be to make money. It should be about something you have interest and passion for. There a lot of genres available in both fiction and non-fiction writing. Before you start writing your book, have a plan of what the book will be about and the genre it will fit in.

You need to focus on a specific genre when you are writing a book so you can market it. Some books may cross genre lines, such as paranormal and romance books, while some books will fit neatly into a genre. What your book is about should be very clear to the would-be reader so they will be interested in what you have written to want to buy the book. Most readers have the types of books they like to read and have a habit of sticking to a few genres.

There are different genres for both fiction and non-fiction books. You need to make sure your book stands out from other books in the same category. If you are writing a romance novel, for instance, how do you make it stand out from other romance novels that are already in the bookstores? This is a question you must answer.

Once you have determined your genre and know precisely what you want to write about, you should begin to think of marketing your book. Make it something that prospective readers will choose when they see it in bookstores or online. This will set it apart from other books of the same kind and lure readers into buying it. You can make a career out of self-publishing your books and marketing them to the right audience.

After you have decided on what you are going to write about and what will make your book stand out from the rest, you can then begin to outline your book. You should write down an outline of the book and the points you are trying to make. Well-written books convey a message. Make sure your book sends a good message to the readers that they can take away from the book.

While you may like the free-form method of writing, which is writing without doing any sort of outline, you must still have an idea of the ending of the book in mind. If you are writing a fiction book, characters come alive as you write. The ending you have in mind may change as you rewrite the book, so it is important to be very flexible. The way you write depends on the type of person you are. If you wish to have everything ironed out for your book, then you must write down an outline that will tell you where you are heading. This is like having a roadmap for a car trip.

Some people do not want to use a roadmap for a trip; they just want to go. If this sounds like your kind of person, then start writing, and the ideas you need will begin to flow. You can amend characters and plots as you move on in your book. Everyone has a different style when it comes to book writing. Overthinking the book and too much planning can affect your writing. Too little thought, on the other hand, can prevent your book from reaching a conclusion. It takes a lot of creativity and structure to write a book that people would like to read.

Read books in the genre you are interested in writing so you can get a feel for that type of writing. Reading is an excellent way to improve writing skills. Before you start to write your book, read the genre that you want to write in and have a good idea of what you want to say in your book.

I

Research Your Book

To write a good book that will attract readership, you must research. Even if you are writing your autobiography, you still must research about incidents that took place and most likely crosscheck dates, names and locations. Research is important to make your book authentic and well-written. Nothing is worse than writing a book with false or wrong information.

Research different books that have been successful in the genre you are about to write. When you are carrying out your research, you can make use of your local library and the internet. If you are writing a fiction book, you may need to research even more. For instance, if you are writing a murder mystery, you need to learn the police procedures and how murderers are caught. You can get this information through your research in a local library or the internet.

Some writers and authors go as far as taking a class at a community college on something they want to learn about so they can be better prepared for their book. But that does not mean that you should allow research to bog you down. Many writers enjoy research so much that they neglect the writing of their book. This is not what you should do. Your aim of researching is to enable you to gather the right information for our book; it is not meant to be used to write a thesis. Too much research can impact negatively on the creative flow of your writing. One way to research what you are writing about is to do the research after you have finished the first draft of your book. You can also do your research as you are writing. The internet makes it very easy to do research now than ever. You can get most of the information you need to write your book if you do online research.

It is also a good idea to research the characters in your book, even if they are fictional. Learn about personality traits. A good writer should be very much in tune with psychology and the way people think and behave. If you want to be in tune with the characters that you create, you can do so by learning a little psychology. Creative writers are often advised to take this class so they can be in tune with the way people think and react in certain situations.

By learning how people think and behave, you will be able to bring more into the book than relying solely on your perception and understanding of how to react in a particular situation. This will also help you with dialogue. A convincing dialogue is critical when writing a book. If you understand how and why people react in specific ways and speak in particular manners, you can give your characters more depth.

In addition to researching your characters and the plot of your book, also do some research on what makes a good book. You can take a writing course to learn how to write a good book or even join a book writing club. The more contribution you get from other writers, and the more information you share, the better your book will be.

There are also conferences and workshops for writers and authors that you can attend. You can make these parts of your writing research. In addition to researching your book, also study the components that make up a good book. For the avoidance of doubt, a good book has the following four elements:

- Three-dimensional characters
- A conflict
- A climax
- A resolution to the conflict

Your book needs to have some sort of conflict right at the beginning, and the conflict must be resolved at the end of the book. This does not mean that your book must end on a happy note, but you should not leave anything unsolved. You must also craft your book in a way that it reaches a climax, which builds up throughout the book.

Another thing you need to decide before you start writing your book is the point-of-view you want to write your book. You can choose the first-person narrative, which is an easy style to write but is limited to the thoughts and actions of the main character, or narrator of the story. You can also write the first-person observant style, which tells the story from the point of view of another character who is observing the action. Or, you may choose the third-person style and still write from the point-of-view of the main character. When you are writing with the third person, you can also delve into the point-of-view of other characters in the book.

Of all the writing styles available, the third-person omniscient, which sees into the heads of all the characters, is the most difficult style to write. Look at the books you have read and see which writing style will best fit your book. The point-of-view that you write from can make or mar your book.

In addition to the point-of-view, you should also decide whether you want to write g in the past or present tense. Most books are written in the past tense, though. Writing a book in the present tense appears more difficult. However, the present tense lends more action to the book.

Research on writing style by studying other books and your writing style to determine which point of view and tense you want to adopt in your book. The first-person narrative, which is also called prose writing, is the easiest style, but it has its limitations. The third-person omniscient is the most difficult style but opens the thoughts and feelings of other characters in the book. This type of research should be done before you start writing your book. Note that you can change your writing style midway into your book if you discover that the style you adopted is not working for you and is not helping you in telling your story.

II

Writing Fiction or Non-Fiction

A lot of people associate writing a book with writing a novel, which is a fiction story. This is not the case today when it comes to writing. There is a huge demand for non-fiction books today. Cookbooks, biographies, how-to books, and motivational books are all examples of non-fiction books that are in high demand. To get a non-fiction book published by the mainstream press, you must be a very well-known writer or author, and you must have a unique idea. You must also be fortunate as there is stiff competition in the mainstream press for authors, especially unknown authors.

Fiction books tell a story, and they have a conflict and resolution. Non-fiction books, on the other hand, do not follow the same lines. There is no conflict in writing a motivational book, for instance. There is a demand for all types of non-fiction books, and this can be a very easy way to publish your first book.

If you are writing a non-fiction book, you need to research heavily and be well versed in the subject of your writing. You should also have an approach to your book that makes it unique from other books. Motivational books are an excellent example of this as there are many of them on the bookstores these days. Think of what you can do to make hour book different from others of the same genre. A good example of a different kind of motivational book is the *Laws of Attraction* series. The author took an old idea, put a new spin on it, and created a series of very successful motivational books.

Biographies do not have to be about prominent people. You can write a biography about anyone who has lived an extraordinary life or influenced a lot of people. Cleverly written biographies about ordinary people who inspired other people are very popular these days. You must have the permission of the person you want to write about or that of their estate to write a good biography.

There had been unauthorised biographies that made a sensation but still required the author to research on the subject. However, they were not given the same respect as biographies that were written with the consent of the individual. You will risk getting into a lawsuit as was the case with Kitty Kelley, who wrote a couple of unauthorised biographies about famous people and was sued by the late Frank Sinatra.

Cookbooks are very popular when it comes to self-published books. If you are writing a cookbook, the book needs to have something different, a unique perspective, for it to sell. Why would anyone buy your book if they can get the same recipe from other cookbooks? One way to make your book unique is to add a bit of the countryside recipe and perhaps some fiction with the recipes. This will be both entertaining and informative to the readers.

If you want to write a novel, you must prepare as outlined in the previous chapter. Your novel should be of a genre that you have interest in, and most of all, something that you would buy yourself if it were available in the bookstore. You can put a lot of creativity into your novel and turn it into something that will stand out. Many people self-publish novels because the competition to get a novel published by an unknown author in the mainstream press is very stiff.

When you choose to self-publish your book, you don't need an agent to help you get your manuscript to the publisher. Working with an agent may be a good idea if you are trying to publish in the mainstream press, but the point is that some mainstream press companies will only work with an agent. And most agents would only want to work with a person who has previously published a novel or other type of book. It, therefore, goes without saying that this makes it very difficult for someone to break into the mainstream press with their first book.

Even if you have managed to get a book published by a mainstream publisher, you would still have to market the book on your own. If you self-publish, you can also do the same type of marketing. Because many people now buy their books online, self-publishing has become the publishing method of choice for authors writing fiction and non-fiction books.

Whether you write fiction or non-fiction is up to you. If you have a lot of creative energy and can make up plots and characters in your head, fiction writing is for you. If you consider yourself an expert in a particular field of endeavour, non-fiction writing is for you. You can use self-publishing to publish both fiction and non-fiction books.

III

Writing Your First Draft

Once you have decided on the type of book you want to write, you should start writing your first draft immediately. What you put down in your first draft may change drastically by the time the book is completed, but the chances are that you will keep most of the relevant materials in your first draft in the final book.

Everybody writes in different ways. Some rewrite as they go along in a book and there are those who complete the first draft before going into rewriting. It may be a good idea to write the first draft and get everything on paper or the computer before you start rewriting. This will enable you to see the direction your book is going and how it looks. Do not be discouraged if your first draft did not come out as expected – the first drat is always very raw.

Many authors who write fiction like to get their first draft finished before starting any research into the book. Completing the first draft does not mean that you have completed your book; it only means that you have completed a rough draft of a book. An average book is about 60,000 words, and a rough draft of such a book may be less.

In some cases, writers will sketch a first draft that is mostly narrative. It contains mainly light dialogue to be put in later when re-writing the book. If you are writing a fiction book, this is a good way to put your idea down on paper, see whether the plot makes sense, and ensure you present a conflict and a resolution to the conflict.

There are two main types of conflicts that can be found in a book, namely: internal conflicts and external conflicts. Internal conflicts refer to the conflicts that take place in the minds of the characters of the book. The conflicts can be due to their perception of other people or the world in general. External conflicts are conflicts that are caused by outside influences. Having misunderstandings with other people and third-party's encroachment into an individual's private affair are some examples of external conflicts that arise in fiction books.

A good way to establish conflict in a book is to present the reader with a problem or question that will only be resolved or answered at the end of the book. This form of conflict is regularly used in murder mysteries. The reader will not know who committed the murder until the climax of the book after the conflict has been resolved. A good book will present not only external conflicts but also internal conflicts. It may also present a series of conflicts in the book that will be resolved by the time the story ends. It is important to create conflicts in a fiction book that will keep the reader reading and wanting to see a resolution to the conflicts in the end.

Besides creating conflicts and having those conflicts resolved, a good book also makes a point. There can be representation in the book as well as a subtle message that the book is trying to pass across to the reader. While it is not all books that contain these elements, they are found in some of the great novels that have been written.

Another factor you should include in your fiction book is foreshadowing. This should be presented throughout the book but should be specially included in the beginning. This will get the reader hooked early on so that they want to continue to see what happens next in the book. The reader will be very anxious to get to the end of the book to know the reason for the foreshadowing. Foreshadowing suggests that something will happen to change the world of the characters early in the book. This intrigues the reader and makes them want to continue reading until they get to the end of the book.

The first few paragraphs of a book are perhaps the most important aspect of the book. This is the part of the book that will either hook or bore the reader. One problem that many authors have when writing an interesting book is a slow start. This sometimes fails to pull the reader in and keep them absorbed in reading the book. Adding foreshadowing in the first few paragraphs of a book is a good idea. Another thing you can do to make your book very interesting to the reader is to start somewhere in the middle of the story. Instead of telling the story from the beginning, you can start from the middle of the story and then take the reader back, through the use of dialogues and narratives, to the beginning of the story to fill them in on history.

The *climax* is also important in a fiction book. You should have the plot slowly built up to the climax. You may have numerous anti-climaxes in the book and other conflicts resolved. The main conflict in your book must be resolved at the end of the book.

Do not make the mistake of introducing new characters at the end of the book who featured heavily in the resolution of the conflict. For instance, if you are writing a murder mystery, you need to have the murderer featured in the book early. Some writers will make it look as if someone is obviously guilty, but the culprit would be someone whom the reader does not expect. You must keep your reader hungry for more as they turn the pages of the book.

While the first few paragraphs, the climax and conflict resolution are integral parts of a book, do not fill your book with fuzz. Each character in the book must feature somewhat in the plot. Every sentence in the book must move the plot forward. This does not always happen in the first draft of a book but will happen as you continue rewriting. Remember that no book, including non-fiction books, appears on paper the way it comes from the writer's head. You must be prepared for re-writing.

IV

Rewriting Your Drafts

Foremost late American journalist, author and Nobel Prize winner, Ernest Hemingway, suggested rewriting a book up to 30 times before it could be right for publication. His notion was that each time the writer goes over their book for rewriting, they would have a better understanding of the minds of the characters. The more you know your characters, the more you will be able to write convincing dialogues and narratives that will suit them.

One important thing to remember when you are rewriting your book is not to be afraid of making significant changes in your draft. If anything is not working or does not seem right, be flexible enough to change it. You mustn't get married to your book. While you are passionate about the book you are writing, also be open-minded enough to see if anything is not working in your plot so that you can fix it.

One of the best ways to rewrite your book is to read through your first draft. You can then make a note of inconsistencies and other plot problems in the first draft. Start your rewriting from the beginning of the book to the end, especially if you are writing a fiction book that has character development. Even if you are writing a non-fiction book, you still must rewrite your book to firm it up.

Try not to write in the passive voice. Write in the active voice; otherwise, it may get lethargic. Also, go over the dialogue and ensure that it appears natural. Look at the dialogue and consistency when rewriting your book.

Don't be surprised if your book has an ending that you did not plan for. A lot of times, writers tend to like some characters and don't like others. The creative process often takes on a mind of its own whenever an author is writing a book. This leads to inconsistencies with the characters and in the book generally.

Each time you rewrite your book, you are making it better. You have a better feel of the characters in the story with each re-write, and the characters become more lifelike to you, so much so that you can figure out what they like for breakfast or what their favourite colour is. By adding personality traits that are distinguishable to each character in the book, you make them more lifelike for the reader.

The more you know the characters in your book, the more lifelike they will appear to the reader. Do away with flat characters and breathe life and energy into them. The only way you can do this when writing a fiction book is to know them. This is obviously more difficult to do with fiction writing than non-fiction writing because the characters are a figment of the writer's imagination. You must make your imagination come alive when you write your book.

Make sure there are no loose ends in the book and that every sentence moves your plot forward. Get rid of unnecessary dialogue and descriptions that will slow down the process of your writing. The best books are the ones that continually move the plot forward, and every sentence has a meaning.

Do not mistake rewriting for checking for grammar or spelling errors. This will be done when you come to proofread your book, although you should naturally make corrections when you spot an error. Proofreading is a lot different from rewriting and will be discussed in the next chapter.

One thing you must do to make your rewriting easy is to give yourself a rest between your rewriting sessions. This will allow you to look at the book with fresh eyes and get a fresh start reading it. If you have a friend or trusted person to whom you can give the book, you can give it to them to critique. They may be able to see obvious errors in the plot that you had overlooked. It is good to be close to your book, but don't be too close. It is helpful to have a second pair of eyes read your book after you have rewritten it to the end.

You cannot rewrite your book too much. There must be a point where you are satisfied with what you have written and the message it conveys. After you have completed your book and feel that it is publication-worthy, it is now time to check for spelling and grammar errors.

Go through your book from the begging and look out for grammatical and spelling errors. There may be instances when grammatical rules are broken, especially when it comes to dialogue and narrative. Make sure you use proper grammar in your book. If you have a grammar check on your word processing application, use it. You can also use a spellchecker. But don't depend on a spellchecker to do your proofreading for you. When you have finished rewriting your book and have checked for spelling and grammar, it is now time for proofreading.

V

Proofreading Your Book

If your book is voluminous, you can proofread it on your computer. But if the opposite is the case, it may be helpful to print out the draft book for proofreading. When proofreading, you should be looking out for spelling mistakes and mistakes in punctuation. Proofreading is a tedious process and something you can pay a freelance proofreader to do on your behalf.

When we are reading, our eyes naturally gleam over words we are familiar with and frequently do not see words that are misspelt. Therefore, it is important to take time to proofread your book from start to finish. By going down one line at a time, you will not be reading but looking for errors that your eyes would ignore if you were simply reading the book.

You can engage a professional proofreader to handle the proofreading for you. They would go through the book in their own way and deliver the final product to you with suggested changes. They will put proofreading marks on your draft with which you should be familiar. The proofreaders will not make the changes for you but direct you to make the changes yourself.

You must proofread your book or have someone else do it for you. If you have a book published by the mainstream press, proofreading is done for you. However, if you are self-publishing, you would not have this luxury. Although many self-publishing companies offer proofreading services to their client for a fee, these services usually cost more than freelancers that you can find online.

Some of the top platforms that you can find proofreaders to proofread your book include Fiverr.com, Upwork.com, Freelancer.com and Guru.com. These sites have multitudes of freelancers offering their services. Check out their profiles and reviews from other clients before you contract them to proofread your book. You can list your project on their websites for bidding. Ensure you do not spontaneously go for the lowest bid. Check out their experience and customer satisfaction which suggest that the proofreader knows what they are doing.

Proofreading a book is not the same thing as editing a book. Copy editing is a different procedure. You can choose to copy edit your book or have the publishing company to do it for you. We will discuss editing self-published books later.

If you decide to proofread your book by yourself, take the time to do so correctly. Do not rush through the process to avoid having misspelt words in your book as it will make it less attractive to read even if the ideas in the book are well expressed. Make your writing to be as professional as possible so that readers will not get turned off. You can make your book free from typos, punctuation and spelling errors by doing meticulous proofreading yourself or hiring someone you can pay to do it for you.

Even if someone else who is not a professional proofreader looks at your book, you will have a fresh pair of eyes looking at the book so they can see errors where you could not see. Remember that you have a strong connection to your writing that other people do not. You have most likely read it repeatedly while writing and rewriting. Having someone else go through the book and check for errors can help greatly.

Most professional proofreaders will charge by the number of pages or number of words. This is a worthy investment that you can make if you are serious about ensuring that your book is error-free.

Even though books published by the mainstream press do have a few errors sometimes, you should aim at making your book error-free. Having errors in your writing can make it look shoddy and not well put together. Errors in a book are a great turn-off for readers. Be error-free.

VI

Finding a Self-Publishing Company

Many years ago, if someone wanted to self-publish a book, they would spend large amounts of money to do so. The press would publish the book and give the author some copies. The author pays all associated costs and fees. Those who wanted to self-publish their book were not considered to be good authors. Self-publishing then was known as "*vanity press*". It was thought that those who self-published their books did so because they had the money, not that they had the talent to be a writer.

The situation is different today. Because many people now buy books online more than they do at the bookstore, self-publishing is now much more respected. And because the mainstream press is very competitive and is only able to accommodate a certain number of authors, it is also seen as a way for writers to have their voices heard.

A lot of publishing houses would not accept a writer who is not represented by an agent. This makes it very difficult for some writers to get their works published as most agents who deal with these publishers only deal with established authors.

Some writers have resorted to having their works published by small press publishers. These publishers would not charge a writer for printing their book but will also not have the necessary clout to get the book reviewed by the *New York Times*. The writer must do all the marketing for the book and only receives a small portion of the royalties.

It makes more sense for a new writer to self-publish and market their books themselves. They can use modern self-publishers that print to order and do not charge outrageous fees for publishing a book. The books are given an International Standard Book Number (ISBN) and are listed for sale on places like Amazon.com and Apple iBook Store where most people today are buying their books. The author can have their book in a bookstore if it has an ISBN. Self-published authors can market their books in many ways.

Since you will most likely do the marketing when your book is published, you might as well self-publish your book with a publisher that does print-to-order publishing. This way, your book will be made available online for purchase, and you will get a higher percentage of the profits. Self-publishing is the way many writers today, including those who have been published by the mainstream press, are deciding to publish their books.

Three good places you can go online to self-publish your book are Amazon's Kindle Direct Publishing (KDP), Lulu.com and Feiyr.com. These are well-known self-publishing companies and print-to-order providers. You can get other services from these companies as well, including book formatting and conversion. They give you a choice of hardcover and softcover prints, and different trim sizes of the book that are available. The books are listed for sale on Amazon and other online bookstores and marketplaces. This is a good option for those who have little or no money for bulk printing and distribution.

The services and options offered by Feiyr.com are like those of Kindle Direct Publishing and Lulu.com. These companies print to order, which means you do not have to order many books upfront. They would print the book when a customer orders it and ship it to them on your behalf. You get paid a percentage of the book's selling price, which is often higher than the rate that you would get with a mainstream publisher, and much more than you could get with a small press publisher. If you take time to market your book, which you can do, you may be making a lot of money by getting your books out to readers.

Look online and find a website that will offer you print-to-order books services. You could get a percentage of the books you buy yourself as well. You can purchase the books yourself and make them available in bookstores and book fairs/exhibitions for self-published authors. Bookstores will accept a book if it has an ISBN on it. Publishers also include barcodes on the published book in addition to the ISBN.

There are now more options open for those who want to self-publish their books. Because of the internet and computer technology, it is now easy for any writer to get their book published through self-publishing. An increasing number of writers are using self-publishing to get their books out to the public who is eager to read them, thereby making some decent amount of money from their work.

VII

Printing Your Book

One of the ways you can self-publish your book is to print your book yourself. You can do this at several different places, although you must format your text yourself and prepare it for the printing press. Online printers will print the book for you. You can get an International Standard Book Number (ISBN) yourself at www.isbn.org. You need one ISBN for each book you publish.

It is not expensive to print your book. You can use an online or offline printer to handle the printing. All you need to do is to get everything ready for printing, including the book cover design. The cover is an important aspect of the book, so it is important to hire a graphic artist to design the cover for you if you have decided to print the book yourself.

To get an ISBN for your books, you need to establish your own publishing company before you can apply. It is costly to pay for ISBNs on a single basis, and that is why it is better to have the self-publishing company get the ISBN and print the book for you. Because publishing companies buy the numbers in bulk, they get them at a much lower rate. If you are writing more than one book and are planning to self-publish and print them, you can order a series of 10 ISBNs and pay a discounted price.

A major disadvantage of printing your book is that you cannot have it listed on online bookstores, such as Amazon.com. You can, however, distribute it to offline bookstores and gift stores if the book has an ISBN. In some cases, some gift shops may accept books that are printed without an ISBN on a consignment basis.

Printing your own published book can be a lot of work, but it works for authors who are on a limited budget, who cannot afford to use a self-publishing company for their printing. It takes some knowledge of how to format the book and design the cover. You should get a good graphic artist to handle the design of your book cover if you want it to look professional.

Printing your book may be beneficial if you have a literary magazine that you send out. It can also work if you are mainly interested in distributing and selling your books personally. Remember that even with an ISBN, a bookstore may be reluctant to display a book on their shelves that does not look professionally printed. Decide how and where you want to sell your book before deciding how you wish to have it printed.

VIII

Editing Your Book

Editing a book is quite different from proofreading it, which we talked about earlier. In editing a book, you need to pay attention to the writing style and grammar when you are copy-editing. For you to be a good book editor, you must have excellent grammatical skills and a specific writing style that you use for your book if you are considering editing your text.

Many of the self-publishing companies offer copy-editing services for an extra charge. Using these services can help you overcome awkward phrases and sentences and other grammatical problems that you may not have noticed in your book. You may say something that means a different thing when you are writing a book. It may make sense to you, but not to other people who read it. A copy editor will be able to read your book with a fresh pair of eyes and spot out hidden errors. They will also pay proper attention to the writing style and correct any spelling errors they may see.

Copy editors will help tighten up your book. They will eliminate repetitive words or sentences that bog down your book. Copy-editing is different from regular editing. Copy editors will look at your text to see whether the words, paragraphs and sentences make sense. A regular editor usually makes suggestions for more significant changes than a copy editor.

It is a good idea to engage someone else to edit your book. If you are unable to hire a regular book editor, you should at least hire someone to do copy editing for you. You can visit Upwork.com or Fiverr.com to get an editor, or you can pay your self-publishing company to do the editing. This can cost up to $100 and above depending on the volume of the book or the number of words in it. But whatever the cost may be, it can be one of the best investments you could make when you are self-publishing a book. A good editor will make sure that everything in the book makes sense and is written in the same style.

Authors have a habit of switching styles when they are writing a book. Most authors have a creative line that causes them to write. It can, therefore, be difficult for them to edit their work the same way it can be difficult for them to proofread their work. Investing in editing is one of the best investments that an author can make.

IX

After Your Book is Printed

After your book has been printed and ready for sale, what should you do next? You should do the same thing that you would do if a mainstream publishing company published your book; that is, promote it!

There are many ways you can promote your book, both online and offline. One thing you could do to promote your book is to get some positive reviews on Amazon.com. If you have your book listed on Amazon.com, you can get reviews for your book from a book reviewing service. You can send them the text in PDF format and have people read it and give it a good review. The more good reviews your book gets, the more it will rise on Amazon.com.

If you can afford it, you can have a website for your books. If you have a website, you can sell your books directly from the website, or you can send the link to your book on Amazon.com to your customers. You can also become an associate of Amazon and get paid a commission on all your sales. You can have a post office box where people can order your book by regular mail. Besides, you can direct people to the self-publishing company where they can find the book to buy. You can market your website using strategies that are used for selling any website.

You can place your book for review on various book review websites. There are numerous book review websites where you can place your book for review. You can also put a link to the book on the book reviews websites.

If your book is non-fiction, you can write articles and post them on article hubs on the internet. Article hubs allow you to post articles online for free. Do a Google keyword search to see the right keywords for your book. You can write articles with these keywords and publish them on different websites with a backlink to your site.

In addition to promoting your book online using the website and book reviews, you can also join local writing clubs for self-published authors. There are many websites for self-published authors that you can take advantage of and promote your self-published book. You should also check up local libraries that have groups for self-published authors. There are also book fairs for self-published authors that you can attend.

You can also send your book to different local newspapers and magazines that review books. Do bear in mind that publications like the *New York Times* and magazines like the *New Yorker* have many books that people want them to review. You have a better chance of getting your book reviewed by magazines that are genre-related to the book you have written.

Small, independent local bookstores will feature your book. So, take several copies of your book there for selling and then have a book signing. Many bookstores would be happy to have local authors visit and sign books with them.

You can advertise your book via flyers and in the local bookstores themselves. As the bookstore gets a commission for each book they sell, they would be more than happy to have local authors come and sign books with them. This brings business to the bookstore and gives you recognition.

If there is a small newspaper in your locality, you can use them to publicise your book. Small, hometown newspapers are an ideal way to spread the word about your published book. Look at your local parks to see if they have anything for self-published authors. A lot of parks departments have book signings for self-published authors.

You can also take your books to gift shops that will sell them on a consignment basis. This is an ideal way to sell cookbooks and other types of self-published books. Do not leave any stone unturned when you are marketing your published book.

X

Marketing Your Book Online

The best way to market and sell your published book is online. Your first port of call will typically be the self-publishing company that prints your book. They don't only print the books but also sell the books on behalf of the authors. You can depend on them to sell many copies of your book from their website.

Tell your family and friends that you have published a book and encourage them to buy it online rather than from you. Send them a link to your book by email or via any of the social media channels. Most websites rate books on sales, so make sure that most sales of your book go through the website.

Many of the online print-on-demand websites will list books on Amazon.com. Amazon.com is arguably the biggest seller of books in the world. Getting your book listed on Amazon.com is like having it on a shelf in a bookstore. But remember that if no one knows about your published book, they will not find it unless they stumble upon it.

Use social media networking websites like Facebook and Twitter to publicise your book. You can also place links to the book page on different forums. You can set up a website or blog and use it to spread the word about your book. Setting up a website or blog and getting a host is not difficult or expensive. The fact is that today many books are sold online. You should not ignore the power of online marketing as a way of selling your published book. Be sure that you do your best to market the book on the internet as much as possible.

Digg is another website you can use to market your book. Here, you can comment on posts and spread information about your published book. Digg usually takes articles and posts that can be "*dugg*" by other people. Ensure that you invite your family and friends to *digg* up the articles so others can see them. The more exposure you get online, the better off you are as regards your published book.

Another website you can use is *Propeller*. This is the Yahoo website that is like *Digg*. Anyone who has a Yahoo account can buzz up a post or article up. If you acquire enough buzz for your posts or articles, it may appear on the home page of Yahoo. You can write and publish articles using a pen name and place them on these websites so that others will boost it up in the engine. This is one of the ways to get recognition for your books online.

You need to have as much online exposure for your published book as possible. Ensure that your book is listed on Amazon.com and the website where it was printed. Also, be sure that you have a website that talks about your book and gives readers an incentive to buy the book. You cannot be over-exposed when you are online and trying to promote your book. You will realise that you get more sales online than you will get from offline bookstore sales. While it is important to get as much offline exposure for your book as possible, you need to concentrate on online sales. Get as much online exposure for your book as you can so you can make sales.

XI

Marketing Your Book Offline

In as much as you have been advised to concentrate on marketing your book online, you should also work at getting as much offline exposure as possible. We have already talked about the groups and clubs that you can join, and getting your books in bookstores to do book signings. Book signings are one of the best ways for you to get exposure to your book. You can do the signing in any local bookstore as they would be glad to have you. You can then bring your books to the bookstore for sale.

Larger bookstores, such as Barnes & Noble, and Borders, will want you to go through the main office to have your book stocked on their shelves. These bookstores will want to see a copy of your book before they place an order. This can be time-consuming for you but is well worth the time and effort.

You would be better off, however, to approach the manager of the bookstore and offer them the books on a consignment basis. They will allow you to do a book signing so you can bring your books to them for display but will have to give a commission to the store for doing so.

You can use a local book distributor to distribute your book to local bookstores. This method may be easier than going through the corporate route where you will be required to buy the books from the publishing company to get them to the distributor. The distributor will then work towards getting the books to the major bookstores. This is a hard sell. Bestsellers from major printing presses have more shelf space in bookstores and prominent shelf spaces.

Just like what obtains in the supermarket, the bigger distributors have the most attractive shelf spaces. If you think your book will be given a centre shelf at a major bookstore, think again. If they take your book, it will be on the shelves. Therefore, you need to promote the book with book signings. You still need to do what you need to do to get the book to the bookstores.

There are many local and independent bookstores available. They are receptive to local authors and will eagerly take your book on a consignment basis. They would be glad to have you come and do a book signing. Look at independent bookstores in your area and approach them in this regard.

As earlier advised, ensure that you join an offline group or club of self-publishers and take advantage of book fairs for self-publishing authors. You can also make up bookmarks for your book so that they can be handed out at such book fairs. The bookmarks should have information about the book and where readers can find it.

You must also do some legwork to get your book out to the reading public. Be sure to do as much as possible to get the book information out to the public. The more you continue to promote your book, the more interest and sales it will generate.

When you go through the time and work of putting all your creative talents into a book, you would want to do all you can to make sure that the book is read. Most good authors are not so much interested in the money they will make from their writing as much as they are in the book being read by people.

Having your book read and enjoyed by people is the most gratifying thing an author can experience. Working hard to publish your book and then having others enjoy your writing is one of the best things an author can experience.

If you have been considering writing a book but are not sure whether you can get a publisher, you should consider self-publishing the book. Instead of trying to get an agent and publisher to look at your book only to give you a small percentage of the profit, you can easily self-publish your book and have others read it.

www.ingramcontent.com/pod-product-compliance
Lightning Source LLC
Chambersburg PA
CBHW030538220526
45463CB00007B/2892